Poetry of the Angels

Eric M. Brodsky

POETRY OF THE ANGELS

Inspiration For Us All

Universal One Publishers
Broomfield, Colorado

Published for
Universal One Publishers
370 Interlocken Blvd. 4th Fl.
Broomfield, CO 80021

A percentage of net proceeds goes to support
The Universal One Foundation.

Cover Art and Design:
Deborah Hill, Malaya Creations
www.onlinecreative.com

Library of Congress Card Number:
00-190623

ISBN 0-9676406-0-1

First printing   April, 2000
10 9 8 7 6 5 4 3 2 1

BIOGRAPHY

Eric M. Brodsky is the founder of The Universal One Foundation and president of Universal One Publishers. These "non-profit" and "for-profit" companies serve to provide love and inspiration through free services and retail print materials. Eric offers inspirational lectures, seminars and group workshops to businesses, stores, expos, and private groups, without requiring any fee. Messages of Love come through Eric for free; it is in this same way that he chooses to share them.

By experiencing these Universal messages, thousands of people of all ages have chosen to replace their frustrations and fears, with greater peace and love. The sharing of these simple messages acts as a guide to understanding True power.

FOREWORD

This book is the first,
in a series of three,
that starts with a "foundation,"
and progresses steadily.
The most widely accepted topics,
book number one will share,
to understand books two and three,
more "openness" must fare.

We share Truth in many levels,
so it may be "Whole-y" known,
each Wisdom "brick" upon itself,
grand structure that has grown.
The simplicity of Our poetry
is for children and adults,
may you share it lovingly,
with inspiring results.

CONTENTS

INTRODUCTION

This glorious book was written,
as a Spirit collaboration,
wisdom conveyed as poetry,
to inspire mass elation.
Some messages are simple,
while others are profound,
listen with an open mind,
for in-sight to resound.

This book is a loving guide,
to find Self-love within,
where you transmute any fears,
and let happiness begin.
This book is our loving gift,
where we hope you claim,
that it increased your clarity,
in the Universal Name.

DEDICATION

To the Universal One,
this book we dedicate,
comprising all existence,
which few can negate.
Your glorious existence,
as part of the Whole,
projected love into this book,
an equally important role.

You are all so very beautiful,
you have come so very far,
allow this text to guide you,
and remind you Who You Are.
Your life may have confusion,
we offer love and peace,
to bring about your clarity,
and disorder's release.

Eric M. Brodsky
The Universal One Foundation
370 Interlocken Blvd. 4th Fl.
Broomfield, CO 80021

877-OneMind (663-6463) U.S.A.
303-474-1734 Outside the U.S.A.
Website: www.universalone.com

Eric M. Brodsky is the founder of The Universal One Foundation, an international, "nonprofit" organization located in Broomfield, Colorado. The organization was founded for the purpose of inspiring people to recognize their own beauty and understand how their love within can lead to great joy and happiness.

The company provides many services, all free of charge, to individuals around the world. This global charity affects all of consciousness by connecting the masses through love and inspiration. It is this Love that we choose to share that integrates Us with . . .

The Universal One.

GOD

The One eternal Creator,
is part of everything,
God is not of punishment,
but of love inspiring.
God is our foundation,
as beautiful radiant light,
equally pure in everyone,
a perfected luminous sight.

Beings are created equally,
God does not discriminate,
all can have this awareness,
yet mind-variance is great.
You can find this Glory,
with faith to go inside,
only within your being,
does this Love reside.

THE SELF

As a Creator extension,
a god you must be,
this God-Self is perfected,
projecting harmony.
To love this beautiful Self,
as foremost in your plan,
radiates Universal love,
in a way only you can.

Many live by other lives,
not happy with their own,
they obtain their happiness,
by results others have known.
Start with your Inner-Self,
it is your eternal base,
a prize accessed in clarity,
pure love you will embrace.

 **ANGELS**

Angels are all around you,
they love you eternally,
call upon them any time,
out loud or mentally.
There need not be a crisis,
any topic you may share,
these all-loving messengers,
help you become aware.

The glorious beloved angels,
like a magnifying lens,
will manifest great details,
and guidance to no ends.
Their messages of love,
in song or in a book,
are communication methods,
visible if you look.

SPIRITUALITY

To be spiritual in nature,
your mind must be awake,
there are no favored religions,
or groups you forsake.
Spirituality does not limit,
by standards of a sect,
it leads to One awareness,
where you Self-direct.

No need to pay a membership,
just live your life and "be,"
enjoy life with loving intent,
great Truths you will "see."
If your life seems complex,
it is lack of clarity,
open your heart to the Love,
that removes disparity.

# LOVE

Love is the only Power,
and God is the Source,
as part of the Creator,
you also share this Force.
Love composes all that is,
as part of the One,
transmuting mental fears,
Ultimately to none.

The only way to know of love,
is to experience it within,
as you become more aware,
"great" loves will begin.
You strengthen your being,
by allowing love to flow,
your cells will be transformed,
into a body that will glow.

FEAR

There are only two feelings,
yet one of which is true,
love, composing all that is,
and fear, the opposing view.
They cannot exist concurrently,
they fluctuate in the mind,
choose love for all-creation,
or fears to be "blind."

To rid your-Self of any fear,
offer Self-truth and trust,
present it to be transmuted,
for disappearance into dust.
These fears are merely veils,
that disguise the loving mind,
by sending love into them,
eternal joy you'll find.

# INSPIRATION

Inspiration is being "in-spirit,"
while fatigue is being "out,"
the length of this connection,
is based on fears about.
Acknowledge its departure,
if rushing or near sleep,
step away and pace your-Self,
for inspiration to keep.

Inspiration leads to "genius,"
glorious thoughts manifest,
Self-thoughts become "reality,"
mixed with your zest.
Whatever forms you create,
allow your-Self to shine,
enable inspired clarity,
partnered with the Divine.

FAITH

Faith is an important key,
to increasing your power,
it is a healing foundation,
where fear it will devour.
Possessing but a little,
leads to inner peace,
large amounts will result,
in mind limits to cease.

Great faith leads to knowing,
which is how you manifest,
your thoughts into "reality,"
True healing witnessed.
Knowing is faith extreme,
there can exist no doubt,
projecting love in this way,
is how miracles come about.

MIRACLES

You are a glorious miracle,
God's love manifest,
a being of eternal light,
that is forever blessed.
You are creating miracles,
with love as your extension,
which increases awareness,
that assists in our ascension.

A miracle is transmuting,
fear within the mind,
which manifests in body,
of a dysfunctional kind.
One who performs miracles,
is a being that is clear,
providing a glorious channel,
for God's light to appear.

 **ENERGY**

Creation is pure energy,
from rocks to the sea,
the difference is appearance,
and the matter's density.
All energy is vibrational,
that vary by their rate,
molecules in "slow" motion,
have a "heavier" weight.

To process any thought,
is energy in motion,
e-motion is projected out,
within the ethereal ocean.
We live in this eternal sea,
where thoughts accumulate,
choose them in peace and joy,
and love will circulate.

# SPIRIT

Spirit is the foundation,
of all the Universe,
One vast connected "Family,"
via Spirit we converse.
The Whole is like a crystal,
each Self a prism of light,
unique in its faceting,
yet One beautiful sight.

Spirit is of all dimensions,
not limited to this plane,
from Angels to the Masters,
great teamwork we sustain.
This Complete compilation,
is where the Self is linked,
varied perceptions do occur,
from minds that are distinct.

 **THE MIND**

Your mind is like a filter,
fear blocks each hole,
peace and love enable flow,
to hear God in your soul.
To master every thought,
is to accomplish everything,
now One with the God-Self,
All-Wisdom you will bring.

Your mind directly affects,
all body functioning,
the balance that you possess,
displays your health of being.
From worries or concerns,
you create much dis-ease,
by choosing love and faith,
pain can quickly cease.

THE BODY

You have a sacred temple,
that is uniquely yours,
for experience and expression,
that your-Self explores.
By allowing peace of mind,
with minimal stress,
you reduce aches and pains,
and your aging process.

The body is the mental "clay,"
passion and love the hands,
sculpting your Masterpiece,
enabling goals and plans.
Length of body functioning,
can never be assured,
yet mental drive can affect,
how long you have endured.

# BALANCE

For every experience,
balance you may select,
for emotional-Self accord,
that enhances Intellect.
When making any decisions,
determine emotional state,
if not over zealous,
wisdom you may dictate.

Imbalances overlooked,
may contain ego or "need,"
one projects dominance,
the other inflamed is greed.
Feel happy about what you do,
enjoy everything,
by being "level-minded,"
happiness you will bring.

 **MESSAGES**

Know that God speaks to us,
each moment of the day,
placed into our consciousness,
where joyful ideas lay.
To distinguish words of fear,
from God's glorious word,
those of love and clarity,
are always highest heard.

Messages are not received,
or often misunderstood,
their simplicity and beauty,
appear to be too good.
By living a life of happiness,
of sharing joy and love,
you are enabling clarity,
to hear messages "above."

SEX

Sex is a blessed experience,
performed as a "whole,"
sharing the Spirit-body-mind,
radiates the soul.
Increasing "whole" awareness,
by experiences you share,
inspires True relationships,
that previously would not fare.

The body sourced as pleasure,
imbalances the whole,
by eliminating the Spirit-mind,
you risk an emotional toll.
Each partner tries to grasp,
a "part" the other possesses,
access beauty and innocence,
with your own Self-caresses.

 **WORTHINESS**

To every glorious creature,
of this beautiful planet earth,
know that your True value,
is of immeasurable worth.
Each being has equal beauty,
not one is more or less,
removed are insecurities,
of trying to impress.

You need not be concerned,
of roles that people play,
all are equally worthy,
yet vary in display.
Enjoy the powerful God-Self,
watch confidence result,
by revealing hidden strengths,
from an awareness catapult.

ACCEPTANCE

To view all in their innocence,
and see life from their "side,"
is to gain a new perspective,
with understanding complied.
We are One diverse family,
that differs at first glance,
yet know that every meeting,
is a sacred energy dance.

When you accept a person,
who does not treat you "right,"
you can be their beacon,
for directing love and light.
These beings have forgotten,
precisely Who They Are,
your light will remind them,
of their radiance from afar.

FORGIVENESS

To forgive another being,
your-Self you must forgive,
the source of inner bitterness,
projecting how you live.
This relates to acceptance,
of the being you portray,
learn to see Self-beauty,
for forgiveness to convey.

Every being is responsible,
for everything that exists,
focused group consciousness,
allowing what persists.
Forgiveness being offered,
without any disgust,
enhances our harmony,
under God you may trust.

# APPEARANCE

Your physical eyes are trained,
to see what others view,
but the only True vision,
is the Spirit sight in you.
Do not be disillusioned,
by how people appear,
they have their own purpose,
of why they're Truly here.

Your vision will deceive you,
listen to your "heart,"
not judging by appearance,
enables love to start.
You were created gloriously,
with Self and mind allied.
by seeing the best in everyone,
more love is applied.

 **LONELINESS**

Loneliness can only exist,
in a person's mind,
for even in a crowded room,
this emotion you will find.
Know that you are not alone,
many seek to share,
as incarnate or spirit,
their love will always fare.

If you ever feel abandoned,
"cut-off" or alone,
bring about companionship,
by loving thoughts you hone.
Self-realize your beauty,
with love and inner peace,
if loneliness is your choosing,
express it then release.

RELATIONSHIPS

For True happy relationships,
to exist at any length,
there must be dual freedom,
for foundations of strength.
Relations are not a mergence,
of two halves divided,
it is sharing of two "wholes"
under One that have united.

As a gloriously beautiful being,
enjoy the Self within,
if a relation is blind of this,
let other ones begin.
A relationship can be limiting,
as boundaries can exist,
start with a Self-relationship,
before others can enlist.

FREEDOM

You may experience freedom,
of body or the mind,
expressing Self passionately,
leaves the chains behind.
If you allow your mind,
to release what you deny,
you forego the frustrations,
you think you "need" rely.

Many people express a need,
from cycles of "ease,"
where change is discomforting,
yet results will often please.
Express your love and passion,
without holding back,
the experiences that will result,
no longer will attack.

EQUALITY

Projecting loving energies,
as equally as you know,
removes discrimination,
and integrates our flow.
Many "want" to be loved,
but rejection is shown,
your thoughtful gift of love,
their greatest treasure known.

Many world cultures,
segregate in their ways,
you may practice differently,
by your free-will displays.
All are equally important,
by sex or job or race,
when people contradict this,
their fears they will face.

 **COMPASSION**

Compassion for other people,
is beauty for all creation,
"sedated" love projected out,
to every denomination.
By sending this type of energy,
instead of distaste,
you strengthen Our connection,
with love you have placed.

Compassion is loving acceptance,
for a being's method of joy,
experiences are their own to live,
their paths they Self-employ.
Allow others their beliefs,
regardless of their defiance,
their free-will and perceptions,
need not your compliance.

To offer anyone kindness,
like a compliment or a smile,
replaces boring gestures,
with love in past denial.
Sharing affects all that is,
of a magnitude untold,
the love that is projected out,
comes back many fold.

Your sharing is the secret,
to never lose a thing,
with focus on the energy,
great power it will bring.
Nothing can be lost,
it only re-locates,
share your love with others,
your "wealth" accumulates.

A HUG

To share a hug with someone,
is to amplify Our light,
which heals mind and body,
where love illumines bright.
There is power in a hug,
it is a sacred embrace,
spiritual love is shared,
as a connection of Grace.

It is a momentary bond,
which varies in duration,
yet the prolonged effects,
are of peace and elation.
This brief period of time,
is one where fears subside,
inspiring blissful harmony,
where two have allied.

THE NOW

To think about this moment,
not future or the past,
results in clear consciousness,
focused and steadfast.
By living in the now,
all beings are seen anew,
no guilt from past experience,
or habits you can view.

With no other time frame,
you Truly live your life,
by focusing on current "time,"
your mind carries no strife.
No judgment of the past,
or worries "pre-endured,"
fears expressed are minimal,
while love is secured.

 **ENJOYMENT**

Enjoy your-Self this lifetime,
there is beauty all around,
listen to your heart sing,
with love you have found.
The elation and the joy,
the laughter and the play,
your inner-child exuberance,
is of the Loving way.

Methods vary greatly,
on ways you may enjoy,
follow your greatest passions,
great love you will employ.
Choose only what you like,
create the time within,
enjoy your Self-experiences,
and let the fun begin.

 **FUN**

Create fun out of everything,
from work to your chores,
sing while changing diapers,
dance mopping the floors.
It is all in the attitude,
no job is "more" or "less,"
each task is an experience,
with pride results impress.

Free-will creates diversity,
each has a personal flair,
look joyfully for fun within,
and express without a care.
Disregard what others think,
and what they feel is "right,"
your radiance and happiness,
invoke their own in-sight.

PURPOSE

All happens for a reason,
perfection is everywhere,
have faith in Divine order,
less confusion will be there.
Every meeting is a sacred one,
a dual "gift" exchange,
each offers new awareness,
where the minds engage.

There are two main perceptions,
"gifts" or "lessons" shown,
acceptance or resistance,
is how each is known.
No occurrences are by chance,
all messages have a role,
offering increased awareness,
for assisting every goal.

 **PRAISE**

To praise God upon this earth,
is to love all creation,
living this way as "Family,"
without limitation.
We are brothers and sisters,
sharing under Source,
to love one another,
is ample praise in force.

Our Spirit is eternal,
our being has free-will,
praise God for incarnation,
to experience this thrill.
There are endless blessed gifts,
that God has provided,
to thank the glorious Creator,
is to share in love united.

MAKING A DIFFERENCE

You can make a difference,
large groups you do not need,
have faith in Your power,
and know you will succeed.
One consciousness can manifest,
anything desired,
from this Self-connection,
miracles have transpired.

We are connected in Spirit,
God-beings within a whole,
there is not one amongst you,
that plays a "lesser" role.
You continue to Self-realize,
what awareness power can do,
nothing is impossible,
only thoughts can limit you.

CREATION

You create your universe,
from thoughts you project,
experiences are drawn to you,
by focus you direct.
You're a creative Master,
with keys to any door,
free your loving energies,
and happiness you endure.

A being not incarnated,
manifests with a thought,
fear delays this process,
while love delays it naught.
Use loving intent and faith,
to start this process going,
where creating in an instant,
is in the Faithful "knowing."

GROUP CONSCIOUSNESS

The gathering of two or more,
results in glorious effects,
more rapidly they create,
when focused love projects.
Envision the awesome power,
of synchronous energy,
created by God-being groups,
"reality" shifts you'll see.

Prayer and meditation,
are practiced on the earth,
where energies culminate,
bringing thoughts to birth.
It is rampant in the media,
with repetitious "ideals,"
turn focus to the loving Self,
to share The Love that heals.

# KNOWLEDGE

Each being can be a genius,
Spirit is the source,
awareness of the Self within,
links to this Force.
Many geniuses from Einstein,
to Edison have shown,
the Universal Mind provides,
All-Knowledge that is known.

Replace the mind clutter,
of encyclopedic "facts,"
with your Self expressions,
of brilliant, creative acts.
Memorizing book passages,
is entertainment enjoyed,
yet True Knowledge filters,
with peace of mind employed.

ATTACHMENT

Attachment applies to needing,
anything you possess,
perceived as loss when taken,
which appears merciless.
When you cease to need,
you can give it all away,
you need not disassociate,
just enjoy it now in play.

The energies that you possess,
can only be re-placed,
for everything is changing,
and is not firmly based.
Attachment grasps stability,
in energies thought stable,
change is like a whirlwind,
to grasp, you are unable.

 **AGING**

To go with the flow of life,
accepting as it appears,
without judging anyone,
you slow your aging years.
Thoughts directly relate,
by chemicals they release,
speed aging via struggling,
or slow it down in peace.

Minds can "deteriorate,"
others blossom with age,
you may choose either one,
let no one be your sage.
You glorious wonderful beings,
your life has not passed,
the "now" still offers freedom,
and eternal joy at last.

HOPES
AND DREAMS

Envision only highest dreams,
do not lose this sight,
avoid any distractions,
and focus on the light.
Fulfilling all your dreams,
are actions Self-inspired,
intent with faith and love,
creates what you've desired.

Dreams you wish to manifest,
are not hard to create,
they will appear more rapidly,
when fears dissipate.
Nothing is impossible,
God creations are we,
place no mental limits,
All-Glory you will see.

 **WORK**

Taking pride in work you do,
is love made manifest,
making deals or raising kids,
are energies you invest.
Great "returns" are guaranteed,
this love is in the air,
feel this "wealth" in everything,
as One in which we share.

The type of work matters not,
it's pride and attitude,
it is your thought projections,
that bring joy or feud.
By limiting frustrations,
it will enable you,
to view more opportunities,
previously seen as few.

 **MONEY**

Money can be wonderful,
for freedom and in fun,
it can assist in pampering,
and reduce all debts to none.
A foundation of happiness,
via money is unwise,
security via the loving Self,
is where it Truly lies.

There is nothing "wrong,"
with money we say,
it is the shift in focus,
which often leads astray.
You can't live two ideals,
for only One is True,
choose either the loving Self,
or that which controls you.

# TEACHERS

The very best "teachers,"
will only provide,
assistance to go within,
for knowledge Self-applied.
"Answers" from a "teacher,"
may not be Truth you see,
their faith and inspiration,
are tools they share with thee.

A "teacher" will manifest,
at the perfect time,
from requests made in clarity,
and thoughts that are sublime.
If people try to preach to you,
that their way is "right,"
these are attempts to control,
follow your own in-sight.

# HUMILITY

When you express humility,
with every conscious mind,
you respect experiences,
and variances others find.
You forego being a braggart,
by the love you send,
your One consideration,
is assistance you lend.

As you become more powerful,
humility will assist,
by strengthening your clarity,
less ego will persist.
Your power may be of status,
or of awareness known,
the use of more humility,
is love that you have shown.

EGO

The ego can be likened,
to being very proud,
yet extreme exaggeration,
is boasting very loud.
You may share it lovingly,
or project it with fear,
happy about achievements,
excited for all to hear.

Allow your Self-expressions,
but try to stay in balance,
humility and ego mixed,
may express your talents.
Excess ego is of fear,
that attempts to demean,
share your life experiences,
with love and laughter seen.

FORCE

Conveying your opinions,
without a request,
may be intended lovingly,
yet difficult to ingest.
There is only perfect timing,
so wait until it's "right,"
force has a reverse affect,
considered impolite.

People are guided to you,
you do not have to look,
many come with questions,
from perceptions mistook.
These beautiful interactions,
increase awareness dually,
assisting you in remembering,
Who You Are Truly.

# FAMILY

Family can vary greatly,
in support or lack thereof,
of your increased awareness,
which provides greater love.
Families are like a tribe,
observing ritual life,
freedom breaks this cycle,
which may lead to strife.

Your family was selected,
before your time of birth,
to assist in your awareness,
for success of goals on earth.
This may be hard to accept,
as most will not recall,
but when this is realized,
great peace will befall.

# CHILDREN

Every child is a blessing,
a glorious love extension,
possessing radiant beauty,
requiring equal attention.
The Spirit in any child,
is no less than an adult,
they harbor great power,
where awareness will result.

Each child offers many gifts,
as numerous as any being,
yet their brevity and candor,
may startle those from seeing.
Children are much smarter,
and aware than believed,
accept their loving in-sights,
as fortunes you've received.

 **ELDERLY**

In cultures of the world,
elders are admired,
for Wisdom and Awareness,
they have acquired.
Acknowledge inconsistencies,
where elders you exclude,
eliminate this treatment,
with a loving attitude.

These glorious aged beauties,
are treasures you may find,
a body may have slowed,
but not their sharpened mind.
Tap their endless beauty,
with friendship and in peace,
treat elders with equal love,
for happiness to increase.

 **INFLUENCE**

There is no one anywhere,
that Truly affects you,
it's acceptance of their energies,
your mind may misconstrue.
Follow your own in-sight,
your-Self creates it all,
follow in faith and honesty,
great joy will befall.

You make life wonderful,
you hold all the keys,
your free-will enables you,
to do as you please.
Go out and enjoy your-Self,
care not what others do,
you need not follow opinions,
just the God "inside" of you.

DRUGS
AND ALCOHOL

Altered states of consciousness,
via drugs or alcohol,
affect your mental body,
where damage will befall.
You maintain your temple,
the creator has provided,
so treat your-Self lovingly,
for whole health united.

You attempt to run from God
with consumption in abuse,
numbing mind functioning,
makes this love recluse.
You can be far happier,
than any drug source,
by allowing Self-love to flow,
where health is in force.

INCARNATION

Having life upon this earth,
is a blessing to behold,
only as a "physical" form,
can experiences unfold.
All should be commended,
for their courage to "be,"
hopes and dreams aspired,
filled with loving energy.

Communication via the body,
is one reason you are here,
express your-Self with passion,
and much love will appear.
The greater your maintenance,
of body and the mind,
the more you will experience,
freedom of every kind.

REINCARNATION

To return to physical form,
once a body "dies,"
you've chosen to experience,
a new interactive disguise.
At the time of "passing,"
spirit and density part,
the exhausted body returned,
to the place of its start.

All souls are equally old,
as the "big bang" confirms,
some have more experience,
from other life terms.
You may remember often,
of previous lives known,
occurrences of déja vu,
are Spirit "memories" shown.

 # DEATH

Dear beloved angels,
that which many fear,
is a purification ritual,
where All becomes clear.
It can certainly be delayed,
by letting fears go,
live a life of love and peace,
a longer life you'll know.

The process known as "death,"
is quickened by the mind,
by repetition of concerns,
a quickening you will find.
Enjoy each moment gloriously,
see all in its grace,
securing this beauty eternally,
in your glorious "Soulful" place.

EPILOGUE

This book has offered much,
in reminding many things,
by experiencing any topic,
more happiness this brings.
Your only True requirement,
while existing on this earth,
is to experience happiness,
where Self-love will birth.

This text is a short book,
formatted to reread,
but only as a reference,
for Self-clarity to lead.
The answers are within you,
accessed with love and fun,
simply do the best you can,
"being" part of The One.

Eric M. Brodsky
The Universal One Foundation
370 Interlocken Blvd. 4th Fl.
Broomfield, CO 80021

877-OneMind (663-6463) U.S.A.
303-474-1734 Outside the U.S.A.
Website: www.universalone.com

Eric M. Brodsky is the founder of The Universal One Foundation, an international, "non-profit" organization located in Broomfield, Colorado. The organization was founded for the purpose of inspiring people to recognize their own beauty and understand how their love within can lead to great joy and happiness.

The company provides many services, all free of charge, to individuals around the world. This global charity affects all of consciousness by connecting the masses through love and inspiration. It is this Love that we choose to share that integrates Us with . . .

The Universal One.

ORDERING INFORMATION

877-POETRY1 (763-8791) U.S.A.
303-474-1735 Outside the U.S.A.

Please send _____ copies of this book as below:
(Please print)

_____ to _____
(qty.)   _____
              _____

_____ to _____
(qty.)   _____
              _____

Enclosed is my check for:

_____ books at US$ 8.00   _____

Shipping/handling $2.50/book: _____

Total   _____

Mail order with check to:

Universal One Publishers
370 Interlocken Blvd. 4th Fl.
Broomfield, CO 80021

http://www.poetryoftheangels.com

READER'S NOTES

READER'S NOTES

READER'S NOTES

READER'S NOTES